Thirsty
PLANET

PATHFINDER EDITION

By Beth Geiger and Greta Gilbert

CONTENTS

THIRSTY

BY BETH GEIGER

PLANET

Each day, the villagers of Marsabit, Kenya, gather at a well. They sing as they draw water from deep under the ground. With little to spare, each can fill just one large jug.

The Wonder of Water

Water covers 70 percent of Earth's surface, so why do the people of Marsabit struggle to get enough of it? We can't use most of Earth's water. Nearly 97 percent is salty or otherwise undrinkable, and another 2 percent is locked up in glaciers and ice caps. That leaves only 1 percent for the plants, animals, and people who depend on fresh water for life.

Each drop of water is always on the move. The water we drink is a liquid, but water can also be a solid or a **vapor.** No matter what state of matter it's in, all water is connected. It constantly moves through an endless cycle above, on, and through Earth.

For example, when the sun beats down on the ocean, water **evaporates** from it and rises into the sky as vapor. The vapor forms clouds. Later, the vapor **condenses** and falls as rain or snow. Next thing you know, you've got an indoor recess!

The rain and snow soak into schoolyards, soccer fields, and lawns. That water seeps into the ground, and also into creeks and rivers, where it eventually flows back into the ocean.

Frozen Water. *Fresh water is trapped in this iceberg in Antarctica.*

Quenching the Thirst

Water has been recycled like this for millions of years. The amount of water on our planet never changes. There is the same amount now as there was when Earth formed. The water that drips from your faucet today could be the same water that dinosaurs drank long ago.

All living things need water to survive, including plants. In some plants, roots suck up water from the ground. In other plants, leaves and stems take in water. On a hot summer day, a thirsty birch tree can take in 300 liters (80 gallons) of water from the ground. That tree can then release almost the same amount into the air as water vapor.

In dry places, plants must make every drop count. A desert cactus does this by storing water in its leaves. Other plants "hibernate," or become dormant, during extremely dry times. When rain finally falls, they burst back to life in an explosion of growth and color.

Plants use water to spread their seeds, too. Rivers and oceans are seed superhighways. They can transport plant seeds through forests and jungles, across deserts, and to new continents.

Some plants make seeds that float. The coconut, for example, has a woody, waterproof covering that allows it to bob along in salty water for long periods of time. When it finally reaches land, it can take root.

A Little at a Time

Where there's water, animals can't be far behind. Water helps animals take in nutrients, get rid of waste, and keep cool on hot days. Sometimes water is hard to find, so animals must **conserve,** or save, water.

Camels can go without drinking water for a long time—sometimes as long as six months. One way the camel saves water is by not sweating. How? The camel can simply change its body temperature during the hottest part of the day. Because it does not need to sweat to cool itself down, it saves water.

Camels are not the only animals that have unique water ways. The kangaroo rat gets almost all of its water from the plants it eats.

Leafy Pool. *This frog mother makes a home for her tadpoles in water that collects in plant leaves.*

Watery Homes

Animals don't just crawl, walk, slither, or fly to water; many live *in* water. So freshwater habitats are key to their survival and that of millions of aquatic animals, from tiny zooplankton to mighty whales.

Some, like most fish, can only live in water. They don't have lungs to breathe air. So they would die if they didn't have a watery home. Others, such as frogs, toads, and many insects, depend on freshwater habitats for part of their life cycle.

Take the poison arrow dart frog, for example. This rainforest frog takes advantage of water to raise its young. First, tadpoles hatch and wriggle onto their mother's back. Then she carries them high up into a tree in search of a special type of plant. When she finds the plant, she puts each tadpole into a tiny pool of water between its leaves. These tiny high-rise swimming pools keep the tadpoles safe from predators until they grow up and become frogs and hop down from the treetops.

Still other animals eat the creatures that live in freshwater habitats. Without them, these animals could starve.

Stored Water. *This desert cactus stores up water during dry times.*

5

Putting It to Use

You need water, too, of course. You drink it and use it to bathe, flush, wash, garden, and probably for fun.

At home, every American uses about 380 liters (100 gallons) of fresh water on average every day. Europeans use about half of that. In Marsabit, where people rely on wells, each person must get by on just 19 liters (5 gallons) each day.

People use even more water to make things. It takes water to make your desk, pencil, even this book.

Growing food uses the most water of all. It takes 117 liters (31 gallons) to grow one pound of potatoes. Livestock like cows need even more water. It takes 2,400 liters (630 gallons) to "grow" one hamburger, and that's not even counting the wheat to make the bun or the tomatoes to make the ketchup.

Water, Water Everywhere

With so many demands on our fresh water supply, do we have enough? Although Earth is not running out of fresh water, it is not always there for people when and where it's needed. Some places have too much water, while other places don't have enough.

In fact, just six countries have half of the world's supply of fresh water—Brazil, Canada, Russia, Indonesia, China, and the United States. The people of Greenland also have more than enough water. Although only 60,000 people live there, each one has access to millions of liters of water each day.

Yet people in places like Marsabit struggle to get the water they need. In some parts of the world, people have to walk many kilometers each day to find water. The water must then be carried back to their homes. Often this water is dirty and drinking it can make people sick.

Dry as a Desert. *Grass is not an option in Salton City, California. This neighborhood survives on water pumped from the Colorado River.*

Use Wisely. *Two sisters in a remote area of Australia sweep out mud from a watering trough.*

Making It Count

To solve some of these problems, people are getting creative. Some merry-go-rounds in Africa use kid-power to pump clean water from under the ground.

Elsewhere, people carefully conserve water. For some Australians, using it twice is nice. Their shower water doesn't just go down the drain. Instead, they collect it in buckets and use it to water their plants. Can you think of ways to conserve water, too? If everyone saves a little, we can all save a lot.

Wordwise

condense: to change to a denser form

conserve: to use without wasting

evaporate: to change into a vapor or gas; to dry up

vapor: substance in the form of a gas

How many gallons does it take to...?

Home

Flush a toilet? 8–26 liters (2–7 gallons)
Brush your teeth? 8 liters (2 gallons)
if water runs the whole time

Factory

Make one cotton T-shirt?
2,900 liters (766 gallons)
Make one pair of blue jeans?
10,978 liters (2,900 gallons)

Farm

Grow a pound of strawberries?
125 liters (33 gallons)
Grow a pound of apples?
318 liters (84 gallons)

NOTE: Figures are for the United States

WATER WAYS

It has many names: aqua, liquid life, blue gold. *Still, most people know it by its common name:* water.

It's what makes plants grow and rivers flow. It nourishes you on the inside and cleans you on the outside. It's a home for nearly half of Earth's creatures and even a sign of life on other planets. Water is vitally important, so where does it come from, and where in the world is it going?

The answer is simple: Earth's water is always on the move. It travels from the oceans to the sky. It falls from clouds and fills streams, rivers, bays, and oceans. It seeps underground and evaporates into the air. It even travels through plants. Here's a surprise: Every time you exhale, you send water into the air.

Water's endless journey from Earth to the sky and back again is called the water cycle. A better name might be the water re-cycle. Every drop of water is used, reused, and used again.

The water we have on Earth now is all the water we'll ever have. There's no more. So it's up to you to do what you can to take care of it.

As evaporated water rises, it cools and condenses. The water droplets form clouds.

Heat from the sun causes water on Earth's surface to evaporate, or turn into a gas. The water vapor rises into the air.

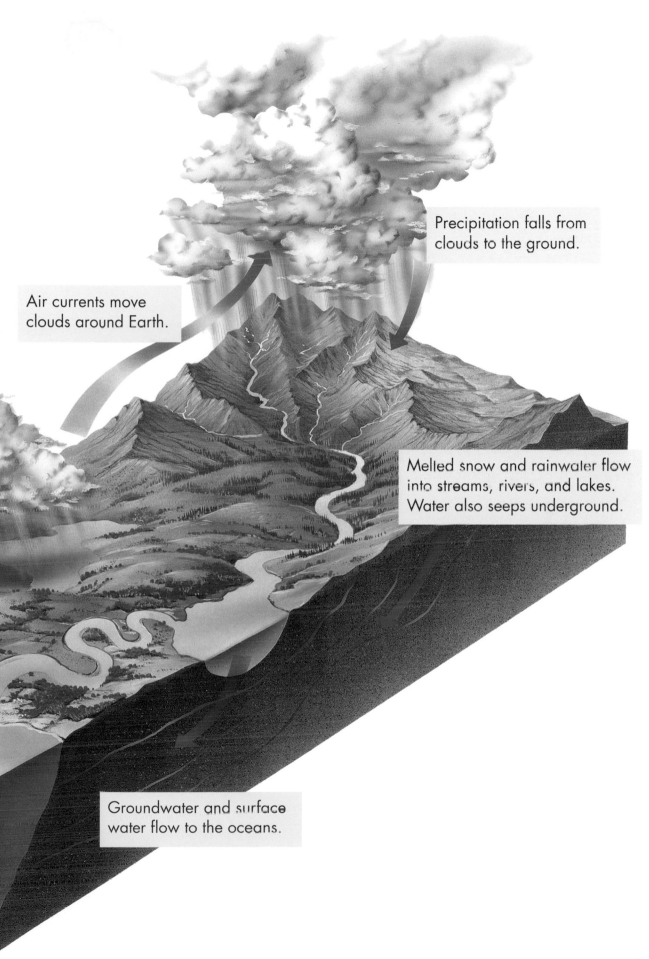

Precipitation falls from clouds to the ground.

Air currents move clouds around Earth.

Melted snow and rainwater flow into streams, rivers, and lakes. Water also seeps underground.

Groundwater and surface water flow to the oceans.

SOME FRESH **IDEAS**

By Greta Gilbert

By the year 2025, nearly two billion people will live in places where water is scarce....

...That's almost a third of the people on Earth today! Still, there is hope. People all over the world are working to develop new water-catching technologies. Here are just a few of their fresh ideas.

Captured Water

In many parts of the world, the water cycle is something fierce. In parts of India, for example, the rain comes all at once, in a giant flood. Today, people in India are trying to slow that cycle down. They capture the water in trenches, before it has a chance to flow away. Their efforts have increased crop yields and improved farmers' lives.

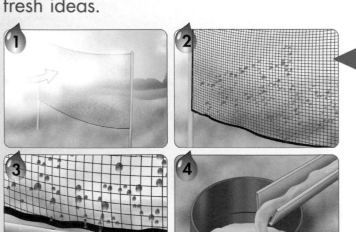

Water from the Air

Sometimes fog is so moist, it feels like you could almost drink it. Today, many people are doing just that. Fog-catching projects are taking hold in small communities around the world. Layered nets capture fog and collect the tiny drops of water, which then travels through pipes into storage tanks. Now that's some fantastic fog!

Water from Water ▲

In some parts of the world, more than 10 percent of deaths are caused by dirty water. A new water treatment method is helping to lower that number. The method is simple: Fill a plastic bottle with water and leave it in the sun for six hours. That's enough time for natural solar radiation to kill viruses, bacteria, and other organisms that make water unsafe.

Water from Above ▶

Have you ever tried to drink the rain? Then you have harvested rainwater—with your mouth! Harvesting rainwater is something roofs do well, too. Roofs collect rain in gutters and channel it into storage tanks that people can access at any time. The idea of catching rain has been around a long time, but lately, it is really "catching" on.

Water Wise

1 How does ocean water become rainwater?

2 What evidence does author Beth Geiger give to support her point that people use water in many ways?

3 Why should people take care of water?

4 Name two ways fresh water reaches the oceans. What other way might water reach the oceans?

5 What have people done to catch water in its vapor state?